How We Measure

poems by

Joe DeLong

Finishing Line Press
Georgetown, Kentucky

How We Measure

Publisher: Leah Huete de Maines
Editor: Christen Kincaid
Cover Art: Jacob van Loon
Author Photo: Joe DeLong
Cover Design: Joe DeLong

Order online: www.finishinglinepress.com
                also available on amazon.com

Author inquiries and mail orders:
Finishing Line Press
P. O. Box 1626
Georgetown, Kentucky 40324
U. S. A.

Table of Contents

I. The Constructible Universe

II. Getting Acquainted

III. Archetypal Fray

IV. Medial

V. Calendrical

VI. Waystation

The act of free will that the mathematician embarks upon...is the opportunity to get closer—from more than one perspective, and by continuous approximations—to some ideal of human thought, i.e. an order and a harmony that reflect its intimate laws.

Federigo Enriques

For the purposes of our study, it matters little whether the Tarot Trumps sprang from the Albigenses' love of God or Petrarch's passion for Laura. The essence of their importance for us is that a very real and transforming human emotion must have brought them to birth.

Sallie Nichols

I.

The Constructible Universe

Zero

Zero. The only place of shared beginnings.
A measurable nothing, like cold—the lack of heat—
or space—the void churned by spinning worlds.
The empty hours of long-past afternoons.
A reservoir of anticipation.

What you can add as many times as you like
without changing a thing. A step
toward the solution, a weightless accumulation.
A tool that leaves no trace after completion.
The greatest mirror.

Gathering

Music came from somewhere, like breeze through the patio.

With temperate weather in late July: nostalgia.

Nightfall obscured the strange erosion of hours.

Chairs shifted to join a conversation, or leave another.

Red candle wax pooled.

Did time and opportunity seem limitless?

Of course not.

We looked at the river.

She said, give it six months.

I tried to imagine wearing warmer clothes.

Reverie

It's a physical fact. If you fly
toward the sun, you will never reach it.
It will keep pushing you back.

That's why it is so bright, and we,
in our ardent maneuvers, so cool—
barely above room temperature.

The solar wind blows—
an eternal furnace—and the sundial
rotates a chill shadow. That is how

we measure time. That is how we know
we are on the ground, and must continue waiting.

Bracketed

I wanted the math that was pure paragraph, the proof that was word elegance, the QED of syntax, the thought that contained the universe. But I could see, in my human way, the limit to my vision. It's as if I were told I could never look up at the stars again. I'd live. But sometimes I would feel a pang of what was missing. I might consult star charts or doodle constellations in a sketchbook. I'd tell people I used to look at the stars and I had some idea of what was going on with their near-endless gravity and fusion.

Order

—Response to George Herbert's "Prayer (I)"

The systems—syntax, logic, mathematics,
a galaxy of diagrams and labels,
subordinating clauses, parataxis,
appendices with user-friendly tables,
musical scales, cosine and sine entwined
(collapsed caduceus around the axis),
tallies of total, median, and mean,
the periodic table, floral taxa,
the somewhat arbitrary names of colors,
thesauri grouping words like one another.

Aliens

1. *Not Alone*

I hope they've broadcast
their news reports and travel shows.

We've looked in their direction, and they in ours.
Somewhere beyond the Great Filter—

new metaphors. Another long history,
and much pointlessness.

If we'd already met, we might
take them for granted, but we're left with

all these maybes. All these approximations.
We're writing down our questions.

2. *Alone*

We might live in the great legend of beginning.
In the furnace of our own galaxy, new stars

are igniting, even now.
Sometimes I look around—

trees, sidewalks, and passing cars—
and I imagine that I'm watching the ancient past—

this will have happened long ago
by the time our light washes over some remote world.

Inherent

This universe runs like an experiment.
The laws hold like gears, like

a cascade of transistors,
like a pen dropping to the floor.

The slight unevenness of the variables
blossoms in minerals,

self-replicating crystals,
and multicolored nebulae

coalescing into planets and stars.

Do we live in someone else's model?
Does it matter?

The sky of a silent world.
The future exists within it.

The observable has a limit.

Million Miles I

I found myself a million miles from my destination.
The world was vast, far vaster than I'd remembered.
If I walked, I could cover ten to twenty miles a day.

That would take over a century—clearly impractical.
But driving could work. Even with stops along the way,
it would take six years.

And flying? If I could fully afford it,
which I couldn't,
only a few months in the sky.

Air shimmering from the jet's heat,
clouds casting shadows like black lakes—
a temporary unraveling of distance.

I'd fly when I could,
walk when I had to, and drive most other times.
And so it began.

Were there moments when I thought of giving up,
of settling down? Sure. I'd take breaks,
occasionally long ones. I'd tell myself

to pick a closer destination. But,
I always resumed.
I couldn't stop. I'd get restless,

agitated, even. I wasn't where
I wanted to be. It was awful.
I'd have dreams about it—

being stuck somewhere, having no place
of my own, not having the resources
to leave.

Whenever I did find a place to rest,
I felt so grateful I could have cried.
And, when I shared a table with others, talking

and laughing for hours into the evening,
it sometimes felt like I could have stayed.

II.

Getting Acquainted

Inviting

I'm not quite like you, it's true—
but I'm not like them, either.

With my quiet steps
and delicate bones, I can move

like the moon behind clouds,
or dash across the horizon

like a winter afternoon.
I can tilt my head

like a beautiful woman,
then fix you with a stare.

Comfortable both looking down
at shallow river stones

and gazing out
from tall buildings,

I'm often waiting.
Will you join me?

Glimpses of the Knack

All around, attendees are talking.
There's something unfinished.
They're drawing it on their napkins.
They're drawing it on their hands.
Some have started to scribble on the walls.
They have this thoughtful absorbed look.
The ink is filling corners
with a stylized lattice.

One person watches from his table.
He's skeptical, but engaged.
He can't quite get the hang
of brewing tea with just hot water
from the water tank poured over
loose leaves in a paper cup.

Invocation

Open your compendium of runes and formulas. Write the symbol for "calm" on my forehead. Write the symbol for "recovery" on my left chest. I want to feel the cool wetness of the ink, the mild stretch as it dries. Write "rest" on my eyelids, but write it in miniature, so it fits on both of them. Write "precision" on my right hand, "resourcefulness" on the left. Summon me to a circle on the ground, around the perimeter of which you write "focus," and I will stand there. Stencil "passion" on the jut of my hipbone—it gives me a thrill just to think about it. And teach me something to write as well. Begin with "insight." I want to place it on my desk. Show me "renewal." I'll write that in seclusion, with a wide radius. And "laughter"—it has its uses.

Gorge

They gorged on tea. They gorged on sweets.
They gorged on rest. They gorged on television.
They gorged on music.
They gorged on self-reflection.
They gorged on alternate theories.
They gorged on sunsets, but
they didn't want to wake up for sunrise.
They gorged on coupons.
They gorged on pulled threads.
They gorged on things that came easily to them.
They gorged on long drives.
They gorged on sceneries.
They gorged on pizza delivery.
They gorged on new releases.

Pour yourself some tea, they said.
All right, don't mind if I do.
Have you read our flyers, they asked.
I had. I was interested.
Good, they replied. We're glad to have you.

Getting Acquainted

Beyond the few sensual pleasures
that one takes to mean so much,

the self is waiting.

The unmade bed—oddly liberating.
The dusty surfaces. The scattered laundry.

People respond to my dishevelment
with puzzling enthusiasm.

Shave this morning? Not me!
Exercise? Done enough of that lately!

But to this day,
no one has been able to tell me
what color my eyes really are.

Hello, my name is awareness.

Is that a name
or just the sound of the
universe happening?

Not the [REDACTED] in her mind, but the [REDACTED] on the ground.

You see, everything we do has different aspects.
You may contain your own opposing forces.

One time I walked into the mall and told myself
to feel like an important person,

a strange blue flame flickering
in the far corner.

I fill the room with shadows, but they evaporate.

The Rite of Something

On this day I became perfectly empty.
In the autumn night, I opened

all the windows and turned on the lights.
My blood pressure lowered.

I looked more attractive—also, profoundly tired.
A woman with a new haircut had remarked

on the dark circles under my eyes.
But a slow pulse sustained me.

I was drained of illness and detritus.
It was a hard reset.

The universe had decreed
I would be known by my new name—

Mr. Empty, the open and unencumbered.
My cares were like May snow.

I had much to communicate—but up to a point—
if I strained, I might become full again,

and we couldn't have that. But even so,
I could hardly wait to begin.

Ensconced

Ensconced in the shared enthusiasm.
Ensconced in a slight mental haze
that nonetheless contains a kernel of realization.
Ensconced in the sudden urge to stand and pace.
Ensconced in the coffee mug, nearing emptiness.

Windows are open. Do I hear the train whistle?
I think so. This far from the interstate,
it's much too loud to be a truck.
The clock ticks. Cool air filters in
from the April night. The new day
will bring storms. And I want to sleep,
sleep within the veil of rain and wind.

Where can we go to be together?
How many years have I been here?
I am the shadow of a stone.
I am the accumulation of eons.
I am an identifiable structure.

The Passage

Where do I go next?
Alternately, when will the passage reopen?
It's been a while.
But I haven't approached it
in quite the right way, perhaps.

My mind has wandered from its logic.
I've milled about.
Grass, stone, and star.
I've scribbled equations that may
be of little importance.
I've lost myself in plans—
the almost, the not-quite.
The quiet miracle. The few amazing
things I've done, will do.
If you don't rest, it won't come to you.
The passage has those requirements.

The river at the beginning of the world.
The river of ice. The void. The sparks.

Million Miles II

Laughter in this café—
three young women studying,
laptops open, straws
in their sweet frozen drinks.
A white-haired woman reading
a newspaper attached to a wooden rod.
And what news reaches out here?
How long does it sizzle across the wires?
How long does it ripple on the airwaves?
Oldies on the radio, board games
popular thirty years ago—
a slow but not unpleasant diffusion.
There's a phone booth too
(looks decorative). I estimate
the communication lag
using the speed of light—
distance increasing delays
by just fractions of a second.

Yes, the sound of laughter,
oldies, and the whoosh of a mop.
So far, but not too far
for the reach of subscriptions.
But far enough that the exchange
is digits and electrons—not what
clanks in the tip jar.

III.

Archetypal Fray

Knot

You decided to become five.
The logic being,
of course, four more than one.
Not in parallel so much
as frequent transition.
We call it managing.
When otherwise the fatigue
creeps in. An insertion
in the boredom. An assertion
of why the fuck not.
In other words, as well,
but also better.

Serious

He seems intense—they said—
and he needs to shave.

And I decried
their symbolic exchange.

Please hear more on my podcast,
Giving Up before We Begin.

It's medium-toity,
with panelists who say "tranche."

Guests include Blur Woman
(with product placement in a tender scene),

Neuro Workers, and Schooner Dude—

and don't miss
our Christmas Episode

on Cognitive Snooze.

MME

Isn't it glamorous to be something else?
An obscure name
makes it all the more exotic.

Like ganache—that thick dark richness.
Maybe I'll go to the patisserie.
Maybe I'll start a web comic.

Mixed Martial Entrepreneur says,
"I'm a Ninja, I'm not even kidding."
Kindness + Violence = Commerce?

The Associate Dean of Calamity asks,
"Is that really how you describe it?"
And MME replies, "You know what I mean."

This is the heart's cry.
This is a dear friend
from an alternate timeline.

Boat Man vs. Low-Bringer

Boat Man said, It's dive bar time.

Low-Bringer said, No,
I'm ignoring your listserv invite.
You're going to be Brought Low.

Boat Man owns lots of properties:
Hum Towers, Bobblehead Heaven,
The Aristocratic Garage.

Low-Bringer has a clear sense of purpose.

Boat Man drove his boat through highway construction.
He would put his name on vanity plates,
if he were into that sort of thing.

Low-Bringer cultivated his hidden talent.
But the forces of culture were arrayed against him.

Boat Man repeated his lament.
Has poetry dwindled down to country music?
Has classical music dwindled down to movie soundtracks?
Has theatre dwindled down to streaming content?
Has ballroom dancing dwindled down to The Electric Slide?

Low-Bringer hovered around the fruit tray.
Boat Man made small talk.

It was one-sided.
It was Over before It Began.

The Rare Thing

A subscription shadowboxing service
and the smallest tornado.

Lost thoughts and evaporated metals.
In other words, exotic matters.

Such treasures are spoken of
in whispers, and displayed

in invitation-only catalogues.
Knock three times and swipe

your credit card made of plywood.
Reveal the candle flame of eyes—

the fire that is a tumble
of glass, water, and light—

which is to say, your casual disguise.

Stir to Avoid the Bitter Sip

I'm tired of figuring things out.
I'll never be Remove Dude,
sporting a Malibu Monocle.

Nor am I one of those indie crooners
(AKA the Casual Wallace Stevenses)
singing about chandelier shops in Indianapolis.

I'm looking for the short commute,
the late sleep, and the chore-free hoodie days.
In other words, the lightly focused ease.

Will you support me on this journey?
I feel reluctant to accept donations,
but they say to lead by example.

That's a joke! Mostly.
Give my thanks to Aaron Bruno. Sincerely.
And a shout-out to Normie Editions. Obscurely.

Momentary Ode

Currents of postponement,
waves of whatever,

a weird, vast compendium,
and the hoped-for surprise.

My self-help manual
is a tarot deck,

my brand
is daily existence.

We manage our conditions.
We look beyond the solar system.

Accompaniment

In his dark coat, the man with dark eyes
arrived.

He moved like light
through antique glass.

He stood with the quiet persistence
of time.

On a divan across the room,
I closed my eyes.

His cadence
began.

What—he asked—
does antithesis mean?

From the weighty darkness,
I replied—

"I am still here."

Million Miles III

They're laying the high-speed rail lines.
Will they be ready as soon
as politicians have promised?

Once, there was a long canal
with many locks, water rising
and falling, as needed.

And above us now, the astronauts,
and those stationary satellites—
locked into place.
Like a torment of stasis.
Or the remove of ultimate renunciation.

Dear _____,

      We are still here. We await. We continue.

IV.

Medial

Imbrication

Lost the thread, the train of thought.
I trailed off. I repeated myself
without the sound of conviction in my voice.

The thread of attention—once taut—snapped.
It was a study in the unrealized,
the inertia of awareness.

The thread of fate, the thread of the universe,
rivers of ice, filaments of dark matter—
all out there.

And the threading of moment to moment.
The fabric of pajamas I'm wearing this afternoon.
The coat I will wear later as I leave, hopefully,
before the sun has gone down.

Medial

Walking the broken fields
near a half-made subdivision.
An early evening of wanting
to get outside before it was fully dark.
A day of wondering
about life's direction.
A weekend of general deflation.
A year of _____.
A decade of imperfection.

What is undone.
What is in the undoing.
What is in the passage of years.
What is in the general fears.
What is arriving or unlikely.

Change is walking.
The houses creak with it.
It falls like snow
and settles on an unfamiliar afternoon.

Change has made its introductions.
So many new people—now known,
but could you call them friends?

Change is at loose ends.
Or is that you?
Arriving
at the cusp.

Typology

The sound of rain means low light,
and wetness
that weights clothes, clinging
to the body like awareness.
Clang of a church bell.
Cold afternoon stripped down to the waist.

Can you change? Do you want to?
Maybe you can learn to change in ways
that you can accept—ways
that aren't really changing at all.

Take questions. Measure your
attitudes, aptitudes, and apologies.
Measure the distance you travel
while lost in thought.

Traversal

While everyone else is still gathering,
I slip down the stairs

and then cross a street
with no oncoming cars.

To the north is a cold lake,
heavy with foghorns,

spanned by a narrow,
impatient bridge.

And beyond that, a vast forest
with open air

like practicing an instrument
when you know no one can hear.

Million Miles IV

They talk about what you would want for a desert island,
a popular thought experiment to stimulate discussion and,
essentially, to rank what one likes best with an added sense
of emotional urgency, of finality, of forsaking all
other options. I get it. But what do you need
for a million-mile journey? When you can replace things along
the way. When you might get stranded but probably won't. When,
feeling bored or sentimental, you might pick up a few souvenirs.
When your tastes change. When you change.

V.

Calendrical

Calendrical

The rain arrived, and for mere moments it poured.
Then came the quiet, the not-quite-silent hour.

A whole new season forms beyond the curtain.
Earthen. Mildly uncertain. Hanging buds
lengthen on the branches. Go set your watches.

Go tend your Solo cup garden. Place orders.
Face inward. Count days until delivery.
Settle into stagnation rich with research.

Late August

Over coffee, my friend explained
she had just gone two years

without sex—*no
big reason aside from loneliness*—

but then became
polyamorous.

It was her birthday.
Later she'd join both her partners

for mint juleps,
but in the meantime

she asked me to show her around
my old neighborhood.

With her shoulder aching,
I carried her bag.

I pointed out
statues in fountains, a path

leading down into the park
with cool air flowing from its shade,

and, at the international market stall,
white and lacey wrapping

on fruit from a country
she hoped to visit someday.

Fall

1.

Despite my love of fall, I
can't quite remember when

the best foliage develops. I used
to expect September,

month of heat and greenery—
call it wishful thinking.

Even October, month of first snow,
might only bring a dash of color.

But November seems too late—
with dark boughs

in the sharp slant of early sunset.
I've started to think of this season

as not a single time
but a process.

Some days are more autumnal
than others.

Summer and winter mix—
bright light, long shadows

in a clear glass vase.

2.

You take your influence from all over.
Sit on a bench and watch. A log.
The shadow of a curled dry leaf.

Awash in loosely emphatic emotions,
you await a clarifying statement—like
the ambient sense of progress on a scenic drive.

You respond to the gusts.
It's both a matter of timing and not.
This is what the season has wrought.

The steam above hot tea on a brisk morning.
Afternoons at the coffee shop.
An evening run—it feels like possibility.

Warmth becomes something not to be
avoided, but sought out.
and the cool is not yet cold.

Sundial and weathervane.
The grand frisson. The heroic heart
you had been waiting for.

3.

The approaching storm spawned over seventy tornadoes in the Midwest.
Curious about the loud wind, I opened a window for just seconds.
Paper blew from my desk. The next day, as I suspected,
many trees were bare. Some brown and a little yellow remained
on the branches—but it was all over—
like a chess player resigning when hope for a victory is lost.

Even though there were stretches of warm weather into December, weather
so warm I had trouble sleeping, the leaves were essentially reduced
to dull brown debris, which lingered in the air as a smell.
Driving to work I had a strong, sudden sense that little had changed.
But I was still in a new era.

The Universe

A landscape appears in my consciousness—
dry grass with some trees and rolling hills.
The light is bright but in a diffuse way,

a thin November sun. It reminds me
of something—it's hard to express—
but it's as if I'm encountering existence—not

through the explanations of others, the rules
and approximations, narratives
running in the background

like the flat drone of a TV
left on overnight.
No, I'm standing in the world,

its openness and possibility,
like a spare melody.
This is my life as only I can know it.

Vigil

The rise and fall of headlights.

The hush of tall, dry grass.

I like to see when things are finished.

Pine trees line the distance like strange hermits.

Full of tangled silhouettes, the land grows back,

but no one alive knows what it means to die.

I could rest on the floor and listen

to measureless sounds, like waves crashing.

Or a noise startling me awake.

It would be no trouble at all.

Favor

Sunday afternoon, driving over
I listen to oldies,

like going to church, familiar
and peaceful in a way I distrust.

A relationship has ended.
As we help a friend move,

the van's ramp
unsteadies us.

Our weighted steps lack finesse,
with gelid rain glazing our faces.

Upstairs, resting from the effort,
people eat fast food and smoke.

Around the corner, I take a phone call.
Closed boxes are a rare private thing.

En route to our destination,
the tarp blows off a pickup truck.

We recover, continue into nightfall.

Snow

Yesterday, skyscrapers disappeared in heavy snow.
Today, the sky is white and light blue and rose
—a pale wash of colors. Smoke rises from snow-covered roofs.
At art museums, I enjoy paintings like this,
and those wintry twilight tableaux, with their bluish cast.

If my lover were in town, time spent in the apartment
would be wet shoes by the door, warm sheets, erotic languor.
Without her, it is coffee, phone calls, and long glances outside.
Plows and shovels scrape. The other sounds
are large and distant—wind, trains, airplanes.

Prairie Drive

At first it seemed like the sun was dipping below the horizon, but
that was a trick of the hills—it was up, and would remain
so a while longer. On the western side of the highway, light—with
a pinkish tropical hue. On the eastern side, night spread across
the sky like a rainless storm. Like a dark blue wave full of truth
as impersonal as gears. Above me, a bright cross-shaped light in
the sky. It seemed too distorted to be a star, but maybe my
eyesight was off. The space station? I thought I could check its
schedule later to see if that's what it was. But then I realized it
was moving toward a distant regional airport. It was an airplane,
but incredibly bright, with the sun illuminating its underside.
Like a game piece made of light.

Million Miles V

Another horizon. Another emergence of city lights,
like a room-temperature star
bolted to the ground by gravity.

Then storage closets. What seemed like
an entire nation of storage closets.
As if for a grand return. Or a grand indecision.

And this massive parking lot
at sunset—preparing to spend the night.
Lavender sky and the soft gray of asphalt
no longer glaring like it would
under direct sunlight.
Patches of green summer grass,
wild seeding.

Cars surrounded me like radio waves.
How many of them were occupied?
I didn't want to gawk.
Some people sat on lawn chairs and drank.
When you made it this far—
well, who made it this far?

VI.

Waystation

Everyone, I'm Leaving

My body can be held. Here it is.
I like to watch myself passing by
in mirrors. My eyebrows rise, as if to say,
surely you're joking.

Less apart from the world, I drew closer to
an immense but subtle happiness, like heat from the register.
If you ask me why
I bear a faint smile,
almost entirely in my eyes,
I might look distracted—
you'd have time to form your own ideas.

Everyone, I'm leaving.
Things fell apart here: the stiff doorknob,
the rumbling pipes.
I will miss drives along the river,
and to those who sat beside me,
I thank you.

The Plan

Like an algebraic structure,
like atoms locked into a crystal—

it portends the inevitable
triumph.

A symbol drawn with a compass.
An elegant response to imagined criticisms.

The people I know
have grown tired of me working on it—

the notebooks, the Post-Its cluttering my desk.

But I have a sense of incompleteness.

I think you could vanish into the right plan—
only to emerge three years later in another city—

not really even knowing what you'd been doing,
as if you had amnesia.

Salutation

Consider my two sides:
the planned and unplanned.

I hoped for more
than dropping papers

on the ground
and calling it math.

I'm tending the store.
Whose?

I'm sweeping the floors.
Yours.

Eternal Lines

Collectors, artists, and start-uppers alike
obsess about their ultimate attainment.
Completist streaks continue—each day much like
another, moment leading into moment.

There are eternal lines that to time growest,
but lone and level sands stretch far away.
It makes me think of jokes whose punchlines go:
it was the friends we made along the way.

And was it that? What will it be? Who knows.
The moment into moment. The yes or no.

Notes
Shakespeare: "When in eternal lines to time thou growest" (Sonnet 18)
Percy Bysshe Shelley: "The lone and level sands stretch far away" ("Ozymandias")

Mixing Shadow

Painters discuss how to mix
the color of shadow.

They want to avoid
overpowering other colors

by adding black.
But couldn't even

water be black?
It is darkness

we are floating in,
darkness that falls

from the sky.
The source of light

is distant and faint,
like the sun

through eclipse glasses.

Anti-Neglect

Elsewhere, things get worse.

Layers of dust thicken. Mail piles up.

The oven burner gets lukewarm at best.

But here, everything slowly improves.

Sprinklers adjust their aim.

Hair returns, as it had in recurring dreams.

Dents uncrumple, scratches evaporate.

A strange topiary of regrowth after long pain.

Not Done

You are not done with that work.
You thought you were—and relaxed.
You took walks to the neighborhood lake.

You watched the leaves show a hint of color,
then a world of color, and then bare branches.
You began to think of other things to work on.

The relief was short-lived.
Still, you wondered if life could be unhurried—
like listening to an album

of electronic music with almost no lyrics.
What do you remember? It begins
as a wash of loose impressions—but then

you start to know what song comes next,
on some instinctual level, when the previous one ends.
Even so, you recall almost no songs

individually. What, then, are your memories?
You see the shape of the music, as if peering
into another universe—but you can merely see—

you can't quite describe. It isn't yours—
at least not yet.

Million Miles VI

I am at a hub. I can feel it connecting.
The axons and dendrites.
The water molecules in snow flakes
with their relentless architecture.
Would some prefer an unhappy ending?
A wreck? Well, this is life,
in all its seemingly improbable
but stubborn continuation.
Bonne continuation, as they say in French,
one of many in the world's tangle of languages.
Bonne continuation.

The Hidden Season

Have our measurements
led to

the true encounter?

Like the washed-out light
of the eclipse—

brighter than expected,
but strange,

with moon shadows
dappling the sidewalk and my face.

Have we taken heed
of our unease?

In the negative fog

of freeway lights
when my phone wouldn't charge—I couldn't

be reached. I prepared
a message, or at least a few remarks.

Have we reached
the decaying forest?

Call it life or death.
Call it rot—and savor its richness.

Or are we elsewhere,
our eyes against the glass?

Acknowledgements

Thanks to the journals in which the following poems first appeared:

"Zero": *Nimrod*

"Gathering": *Mantis*

"Aliens": *Redactions*

"Glimpses of the Knack": *Cimarron Review*

"Boat Man vs. Low-Bringer": *Denver Quarterly*

"Favor": *Roanoke Review*

"Everyone, I'm Leaving": *Puerto del Sol*

Thanks to those who've shaped my journey with literature: David Citino, John Drury, Andrew Hudgins, Erin McGraw, Don Bogen, Lisa Hogeland, Jon Kamholtz, George Scott Revis, Mike Geer, Karen Craigo, Bimini Folger, Leith Morton, Noriko Hara, Ken'ichi Sasō, Mark Levine, Aron Aji, and Jan Steyn.

Thanks to those who've shown me friendship and hospitality over the years: Chris Hammond, Joey Brinkmeier, Josh Butts, Lesley Jenike, Hannah Reck, Byron Bailey, Neely McLaughlin, Annie Pécastaings, Mary Assad, Hee-Seung Kang, Gusztav Demeter, Ana Codita, Lizzie Buehler, Adrian Demopulos, and Claire Dockery.

And special thanks to Ruth Williams for her companionship, my sister Lisa DeLong for her creative siblingship, and my mother Rebecca DeLong for her boundless love and support.

J oe DeLong was born in Ohio and has lived in many of its major cities (Dayton, Columbus, Cincinnati, and Cleveland). He has an MFA in literary translation from the University of Iowa and a PhD in English from the University of Cincinnati. In addition to his poetry, he has published translations (with Noriko Hara) of Japanese poet Ken'ichi Sasō in journals such as *Asymptote*, *Two Lines*, and *Painted Bride Quarterly*. His other publications include visual poetry (a combination of original illustrations and text), as well as scholarly articles on memoirs by mathematicians and the contemporary poetry of Quebec. He teaches in the Program in Technical Communication at the University of Michigan.

www.ingramcontent.com/pod-product-compliance
Lightning Source LLC
Chambersburg PA
CBHW021157090426
42740CB00008B/1134